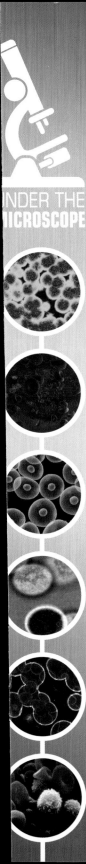

CELLS
UP CLOSE

Gareth Stevens
Publishing

BY MARIA NELSON

Please visit our website, www.garethstevens.com. For a free color catalog of all our high-quality books, call toll free 1-800-542-2595 or fax 1-877-542-2596.

Library of Congress Cataloging-in-Publication Data

Nelson, Maria.
Cells up close / Maria Nelson.
    pages cm. — (Under the microscope)
Includes bibliographical references and index.
ISBN 978-1-4339-8339-9 (pbk.)
ISBN 978-1-4339-8340-5 (6-pack)
ISBN 978-1-4339-8338-2 (library binding)
1. Cells—Juvenile literature. 2. Cytology—Juvenile literature. 3. Microscopy—Juvenile literature. I. Title.
QH582.5.N45 2014
571.6—dc23

                                   2012047098

First Edition

Published in 2014 by
Gareth Stevens Publishing
111 East 14th Street, Suite 349
New York, NY 10003

Copyright © 2014 Gareth Stevens Publishing

Designer: Katelyn E. Reynolds
Editor: Therese Shea

Photo credits: Cover, p. 1 Kenneth Eward/Photo Researchers/Getty Images; cover, pp. 1, 3–31 (logo and cells image icons) iStockphoto/Thinkstock.com; cover, pp. 1–31 (cell image icon) Chad Baker/Photodisc/Thinkstock.com; cover, pp. 1–32 (background texture and cell image icon) Hemera/Thinkstock.com; p. 5 (cells inset) © iStockphoto.com/Henrik5000; p. 5 (main image) Brand X Pictures/Thinkstock.com; p. 7 Photo Researchers/Getty Images; p. 8 Dr. T.J. Beveridge/Visuals Unlimited/Getty Images; p. 9 Dr. Donald Fawcett/Visuals Unlimited/Getty Images; p. 11 Biophoto Associates/Photo Researchers/Getty Images; p. 12 CNRI/Science Photo Library/Getty Images; p. 13 Dorling Kindersley/Getty Images; p. 14 Encyclopaedia Britannica/Universal Images Group/Getty Images; p. 15 Materialscientist/Wikipedia.com; p. 16 iStockphoto/Thinkstock.com; p. 17 Ed Reschke/Peter Arnold/Getty Images; p. 18 Dorling Kindersely RF/Thinkstock.com; p. 19 Garry DeLong/Oxford Scientific/Getty Images; pp. 20, 29 Getty Images; pp. 21, 28 Anne-Christine Poujoulat/AFP/Getty Images; p. 23 Jupiterimages/liquidlibrary/Thinkstock.com; p. 25 Hemera/Thinkstock.com; p. 27 (main) Ingram Publishing/Thinkstock.com; p. 27 (inset) George Whitely/Photo Researchers/Getty Images.

Printed in the United States of America

CPSIA compliance information: Batch #CS13GS: For further information contact Gareth Stevens, New York, New York at 1-800-542-2595.

CONTENTS

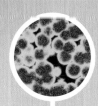

Words in the glossary appear in **bold** type the first time they are used in the text.

YOU, ON THE CELLULAR LEVEL

DID YOU KNOW?

Biology is the study of life. The study of cells is part of microbiology. "Micro" is from a Greek word meaning "small."

Have you ever wondered what you're made of? When you look in the mirror, you can see how different your skin looks from your teeth. And your hair doesn't resemble your eyeballs at all! Despite how different they look, all your body parts—inside and out—are made up of the same units: cells.

Cells are the basic unit of life. They're so small that most can only be seen with a microscope. Organelles are even smaller parts within cells. All living things, or organisms, are made up of cells. While the human body is made up of between 75 trillion and 100 trillion cells, there are also organisms all around us made up of just one cell. But are the cells of every organism the same?

HOW SMALL
IS IT?

Cells are so tiny that scientists have to measure them using micrometers. A micrometer is equal to 0.000039 inch. A human cell is about 20 micrometers across, or 0.00078 inch. How small is this? It would take about 10,000 human cells to cover the tip of your pen! The smallest single-celled organism, from a group of **bacteria** called mycoplasmas, is only about 0.3 micrometer across.

You are made up of cells. Those cells are made up of the building blocks of all matter, atoms.

PROKARYOTES
AND EUKARYOTES

Scientists divide cells into two main groups. Prokaryotes include bacteria and other small organisms called archaeans. Plants, fungi, **protists**, and animals—including humans—are eukaryotes. A eukaryotic cell is often just a part of a larger organism. But a prokaryotic cell is the organism! Prokaryotes are also called single-celled or unicellular organisms. The most common unicellular organisms are the most common organisms on Earth—bacteria.

While eukaryotic cells are more complex than prokaryotic cells, their basic structure is similar. All cells have a surrounding casing that holds in the cell's other parts. They're filled with fluid and most contain **genetic** material, or DNA. Prokaryotic and eukaryotic cells also carry out many of the same functions, including dividing to create more cells and getting rid of waste.

A GREAT DISCOVERY

Scientists began studying the smallest parts of living things using some of the first microscopes more than 400 years ago. At least one of them, British scientist Nehemiah Grew, observed cells but didn't know how important they were. Robert Hooke, another British scientist, saw tiny, boxlike structures in a piece of cork. He called these structures "cells." Hooke also found cells in trees and other plants. He guessed they helped move matter through plants.

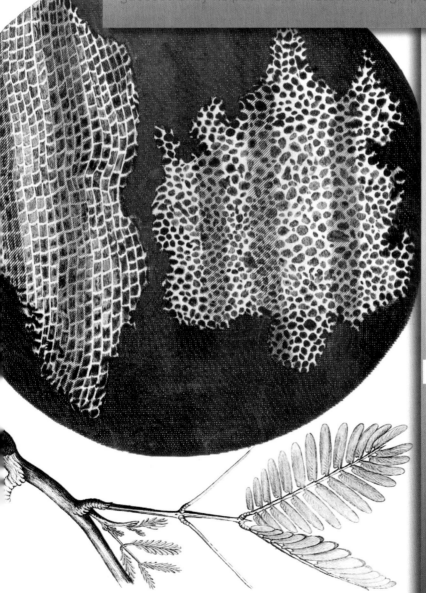

This is a drawing of the cells of a corkwood tree.

DNA JUMBLE

When you look at a bacterium under a microscope, it has something in the middle of it that looks somewhat like a balled-up piece of string. This is the bacterium's DNA. It's only kept from the outside world by the cell **membrane**. Considering how tiny a bacterium cell is, it sure holds a lot of genetic material. If you stretched out the "string" of a bacterium's DNA, it would be about 1,000 times longer than the cell itself!

You can see the difference between the prokaryotic and eukaryotic cells in these photos. The prokaryote's "nucleoid," or the area where its DNA is held, has no membrane.

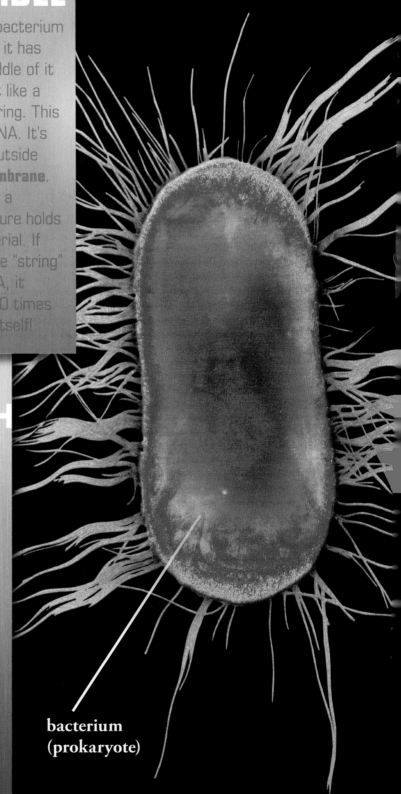

bacterium
(prokaryote)

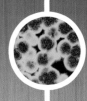

Prokaryotic and eukaryotic cells look different under a microscope, especially if you know what to look for. For example, some bacteria cells are shaped like capsules and others like spirals. Some have taillike structures called flagella that help them move. However, a key way to tell the difference between eukaryotic and prokaryotic cells under the microscope is finding their genetic material. Eukaryotic cells have a nucleus surrounded by a membrane. Prokaryotes don't.

Another major difference between prokaryotes and eukaryotes is how they relate to each other. Bacteria cells may live together in a colony, also called a filament. However, each of these cells operates independently. Eukaryotic cells often work together within an organism. They may differentiate, or become different kinds of cells as they grow.

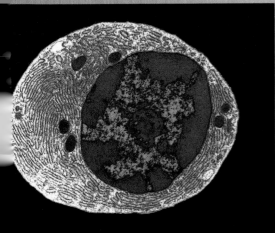

The nucleus of the eukaryote is contained in a membrane.

WHAT'S IN A CELL?

DID YOU KNOW?

Lipids are made up of chains of molecules called fatty acids. In addition to building cell membranes, they're an important way organisms store energy.

Since DNA is the blueprint that gives a cell its form and tells it what to do, the nucleus might be the most important organelle in a eukaryotic cell. Whether animal, plant, or protist, a cell needs this information to function. That's why the DNA is contained by a nuclear envelope, or membrane, that keeps it separate from the other parts of the cell.

The cell's first line of defense, however, is the outer membrane. Both eukaryotic and prokaryotic cells have this membrane. In a eukaryote, it's called a plasma membrane, while in a prokaryote it's called a cell membrane. It's made of **proteins** and fat molecules called lipids. The membrane allows needed matter into the cell and keeps harmful matter out. Cell waste also moves out through the membrane.

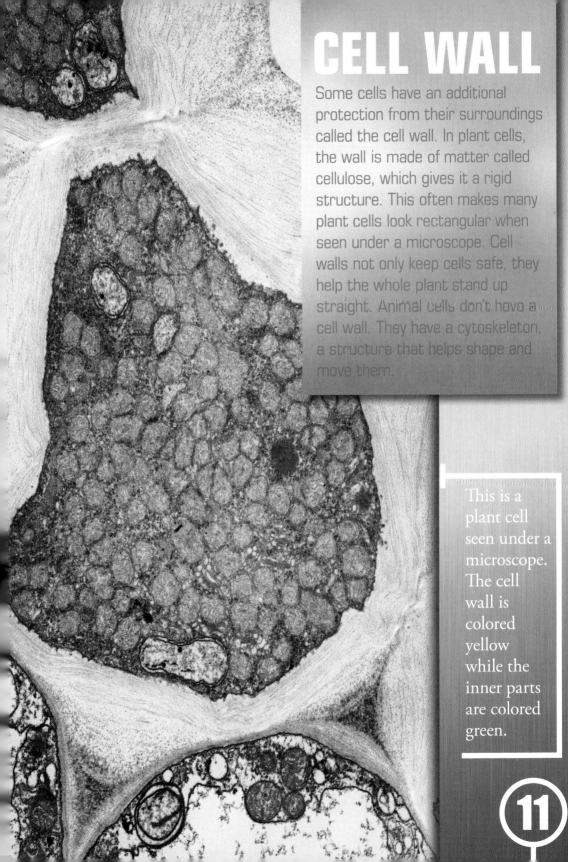

CELL WALL

Some cells have an additional protection from their surroundings called the cell wall. In plant cells, the wall is made of matter called cellulose, which gives it a rigid structure. This often makes many plant cells look rectangular when seen under a microscope. Cell walls not only keep cells safe, they help the whole plant stand up straight. Animal cells don't have a cell wall. They have a cytoskeleton, a structure that helps shape and move them.

This is a plant cell seen under a microscope. The cell wall is colored yellow while the inner parts are colored green.

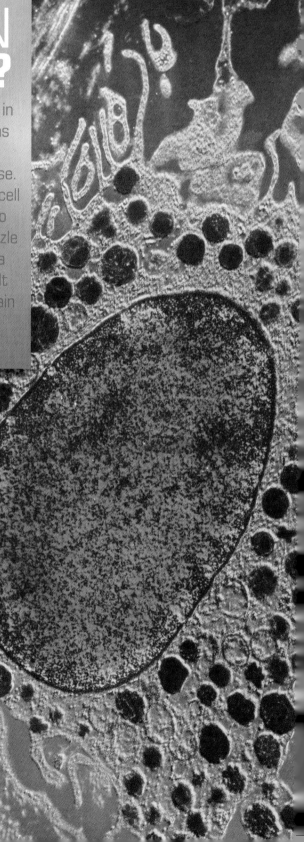

WHAT CAN ENZYMES DO?

Enzymes do most of the hard work in the cell. They use chemical reactions to either break down or combine molecules into forms the cell can use. Enzymes can make lipids to fix the cell membrane or break down foods into **nutrients**. Think of enzymes like puzzle pieces. Each one has a shape with a special space called an active site. It uses the active site to bind to certain molecules and perform a chemical reaction on them.

What looks like open space in this cell is actually full of cytoplasm and enzymes at work!

The inner space of a cell is filled with fluid called cytoplasm. It has many jobs, one of which is to help the cell break down waste. Cytoplasm also moves matter around the cell. In eukaryotic cells, the cytoplasm is sometimes called the "soup" that holds all the organelles. In prokaryotic cells, it's where the DNA resides.

Using a microscope, it's easy to see the cytoplasm-filled spaces of a cell. Perhaps the most important parts of the cytoplasm are so small they can squeeze through pathways in the cell's membranes! These molecules are called enzymes and are made of proteins produced by the cell. There may be hundreds or millions of copies of an enzyme in a cell, depending on the importance of its job.

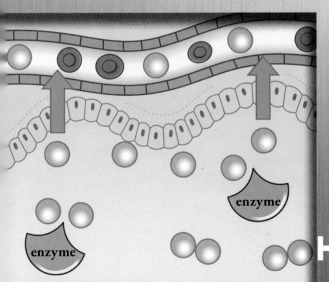

In this drawing, enzymes move molecules in the digestive system.

LITTLE ORGANS

The term "organelle" means "little organ." In eukaryotic cells, each organelle is protected by its own membrane. Cells may have different numbers of each type of organelle. For example, a cell can have hundreds or thousands of ribosomes in it. However, each cell only has one nucleus. The term "eukaryote" means "true nucleus." Some scientists guess that organelles called mitochondria were once prokaryotes! Keep reading to learn more about mitochondria, the cell's energy factory.

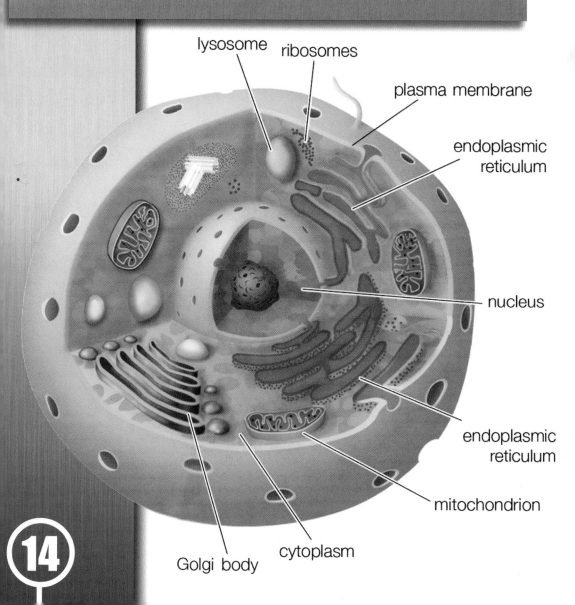

lysosome
ribosomes
plasma membrane
endoplasmic reticulum
nucleus
endoplasmic reticulum
mitochondrion
Golgi body
cytoplasm

Depending on the kind it is, a cell may contain several organelles to carry out important functions.

- Ribosomes are found in both eukaryotic and prokaryotic cells. They make proteins.

- Endoplasmic reticulum, or ER, moves molecules around the cell. Some parts of ER have ribosomes attached to them, and the ER helps move the proteins made by ribosomes.

- The Golgi body acts much like a post office. It takes in, packages, and transports some proteins.

- Lysosomes are structures with special enzymes that break down molecules into waste, including damaged organelles or bacteria that enter the cell.

- Vacuoles are found in plant and fungi cells. Along with smaller organelles called vesicles, they're used for storage and chemical movement.

DID YOU KNOW?

The Golgi body is named after the scientist who discovered it, Camillo Golgi.

This is a drawing of a eukaryotic cell. You can see its many organelles.

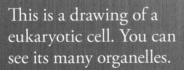

THE POWERHOUSES

When you have a snack, you might be looking for a little energy boost. Did you know that the energy you get from your banana or sandwich comes from processes in cells?

Eukaryotic cells use organelles called mitochondria to break down glucose, a kind of sugar you get from your food. Glucose is then converted into energy. Mitochondria have an outer membrane that encloses them and a folded inner membrane, too. They also have a small bit of special DNA that helps them make proteins.

Plant cells have additional energy-producing organelles called chloroplasts. These structures are similar to mitochondria. However, chloroplasts use photosynthesis, a process that converts sunlight and carbon dioxide to energy, rather than breaking down food.

mitochondrion

SOLAR-POWERED PLANTS

Chloroplasts need chlorophyll, a green **pigment**, for photosynthesis. It's important for plants to have mitochondria, too, in case they don't get enough sunlight for photosynthesis to occur. Chloroplasts can be seen using a microscope, but photosynthesis is harder to observe. That's because it's a chemical process. It can be written out like this:

$$\text{carbon dioxide} + \text{water} \xrightarrow[\text{chlorophyll}]{\text{sunlight}} \text{glucose} + \text{oxygen}$$

The green structures within these plant cells are chloroplasts.

DIFFERENTIATION

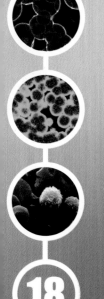

DID YOU KNOW?

Mammals have more than 200 kinds of cells in their bodies.

Look at yourself in the mirror again. If your whole body is made of cells, why don't your earlobes look like the inside of your stomach? When eukaryotic cells are part of a larger organism, they differentiate, or become specialized.

In humans, differentiation is ongoing. A baby couldn't grow inside its mother without it. All your body's cells began from just one that continued to divide until it became you! Parts of a cell's DNA are turned "on" or "off" to make it become part of a kidney, leg bone, skin, or other body part. Cells then specialize further. Even among one tissue or organ's specialized cells, there must be different cells to perform the functions of each part. The cells from your various body parts look somewhat different under a microscope.

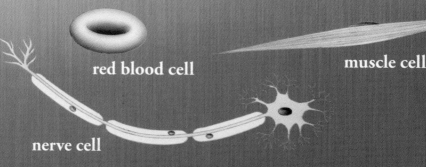

red blood cell

muscle cell

nerve cell

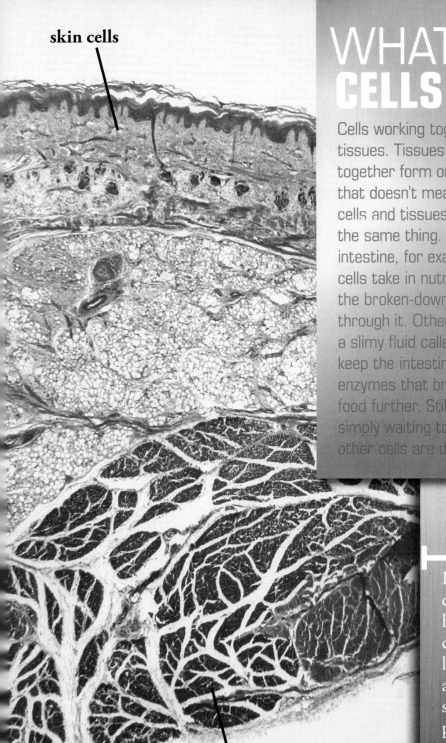

skin cells

muscle cells

WHAT DO CELLS DO?

Cells working together form tissues. Tissues working together form organs. But that doesn't mean all these cells and tissues are doing the same thing. In your small intestine, for example, some cells take in nutrients from the broken-down food moving through it. Others **secrete** a slimy fluid called mucus to keep the intestines slick or enzymes that break down food further. Still more are simply waiting to take over if other cells are damaged.

Differentiated cells of the human body created the layers of skin and muscle seen in this photo.

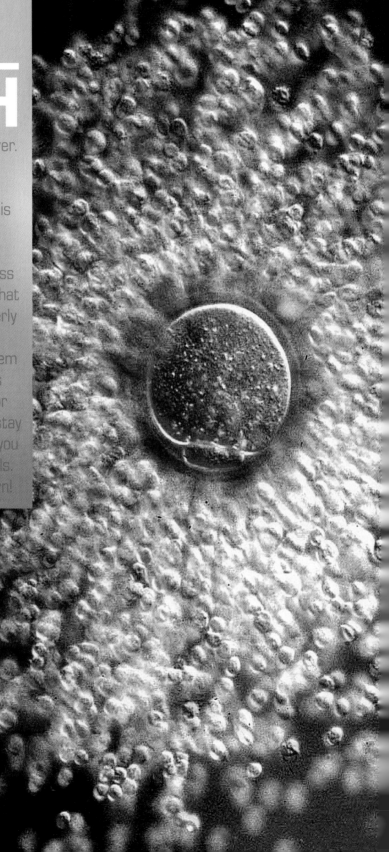

CELL
DEATH

Cells don't live forever. If a cell is damaged or infected, it may allow itself to die. This is called apoptosis. Apoptosis is an important cell process since it stops cells that aren't working properly from dividing and creating more problem cells. However, cells can also be killed. For example, when you stay in the sun too long, you may kill your skin cells. We call that sunburn!

A germ-line cell is surrounded by many somatic cells in this photo.

While differentiation creates many kinds of cells, human cells are grouped into three main types. The largest group is somatic cells—those that make up body parts such as skin and muscle.

Germ-line cells make up a human's gametes, or the special cells used in reproduction. Gametes differ from other cells in an important way. They only have half the amount of genetic material. That's because two kinds of gametes—one from a male and one from a female—are needed to make the cell that will become an organism. This is the cell from which all other body cells arise.

Stem cells are cells that haven't differentiated yet. Many scientists want to study them to find out if they can help people with diseases.

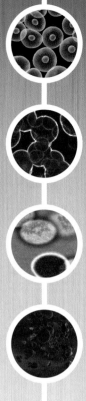

DID YOU KNOW?

There's a lot of **debate** about the use of stem cells. Some people think using some kinds of stem cells should be illegal.

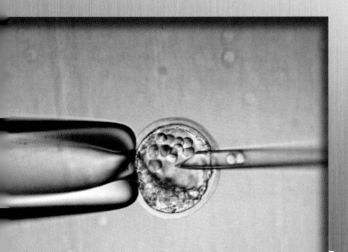

stem cell

LET'S MULTIPLY!

DID YOU KNOW?

A few organisms reproduce by budding, a process in which a new cell grows out from another cell, like a bud. After the bud is formed, DNA is copied and passed into it. Then, the bud splits off.

Cell division is vital to the survival of all kinds of organisms. In unicellular organisms, cell division creates more of that kind of organism. Cell division helps multicellular organisms to grow and repair themselves. There are a few ways cells divide.

Most prokaryotes reproduce by binary fission. The similar process in eukaryotes is called mitosis. In both, the cell makes a copy of its DNA. Then it splits in two with one copy of the DNA in each cell.

Some eukaryotes have another process of cell reproduction. Cells divide to produce gametes in a process called meiosis. However, each cell has only half the DNA. When a male gamete meets a female gamete, they combine to make a complete set of DNA.

CANCER

Sometimes, the body's growth control systems don't operate properly. Cells may divide uncontrollably. This is a main feature of the disease called cancer. Cancerous cell growth starts with a single cell that has damaged DNA. Usually, the kind of DNA damage that causes healthy cells to become cancer cells takes a long time to occur. It can be inherited, caused by the conditions in a person's body, or just happen during cell division.

In the center cell in this photo, you can see the cell splitting its DNA, getting ready for cell division.

THE BODY'S BLUEPRINT

From directing the production of enzymes to determining what color a person's eyes will be, the DNA inside a cell has varied and important jobs. And thanks to very powerful microscopes, we can see it up close! DNA in a human cell looks much different from the wadded-up string found in bacteria. We have so much DNA that it's packed into tight bundles called chromosomes to fit into our cells.

In 1953, scientists James Watson and Francis Crick made a model of human DNA called the double helix. It helped explain how our DNA copies itself to make more DNA. We now know that DNA is made up of only four different kinds of molecules called nucleotides that repeat in different patterns. Their order is a kind of code that tells a cell what to do.

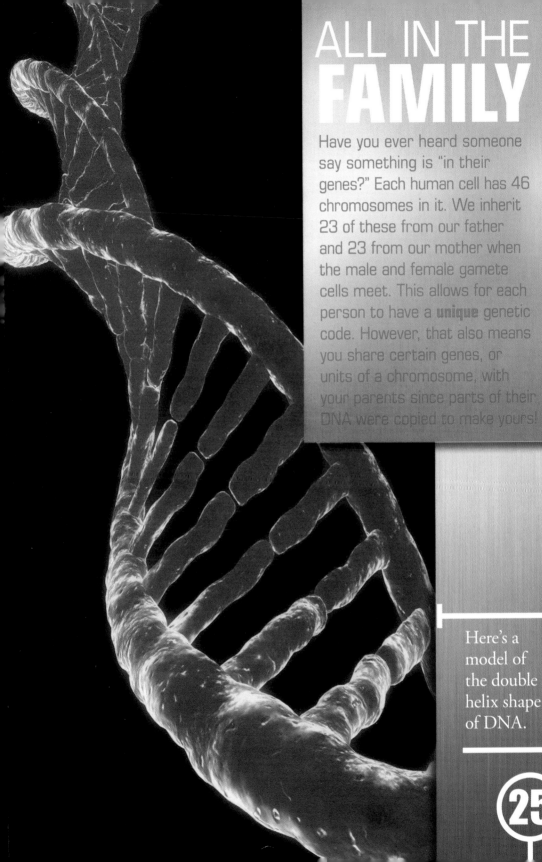

ALL IN THE
FAMILY

Have you ever heard someone say something is "in their genes?" Each human cell has 46 chromosomes in it. We inherit 23 of these from our father and 23 from our mother when the male and female gamete cells meet. This allows for each person to have a **unique** genetic code. However, that also means you share certain genes, or units of a chromosome, with your parents since parts of their DNA were copied to make yours!

Here's a model of the double helix shape of DNA.

SEEING CELLS

In 2011, a group of scientists in England started using a microscope powerful enough to study the parts of a human cell. Called the microsphere nanoscope, it allowed them to see tiny details 20 times smaller than any previous microscopes!

The microsphere nanoscope is an optical microscope, also called a light microscope. If you have used a microscope in science class, it was probably an optical microscope, though a much simpler model than the microsphere nanoscope. Optical microscopes use light and lenses to magnify objects. Scientists also use **electron** microscopes. Instead of light, these microscopes use electrons to show an image of a **specimen**. While these tools have powerful magnifying abilities, electron microscopes cannot observe live cells in action. Optical microscopes can!

CELLS IN FOCUS

When using optical microscopes, scientists need ways to make details of a cell stand out. They may use staining, or adding dye to a specimen, as a way to add contrast. They also use special optical microscopes called dark-field light microscopes. These tools block light so that the cell lights up against a black background. Both methods allow fine details to stand out. When using the microsphere nanoscope, though, neither of these is needed.

This optical microscope uses light and a variety of lenses to help a scientist magnify a specimen of blood cells.

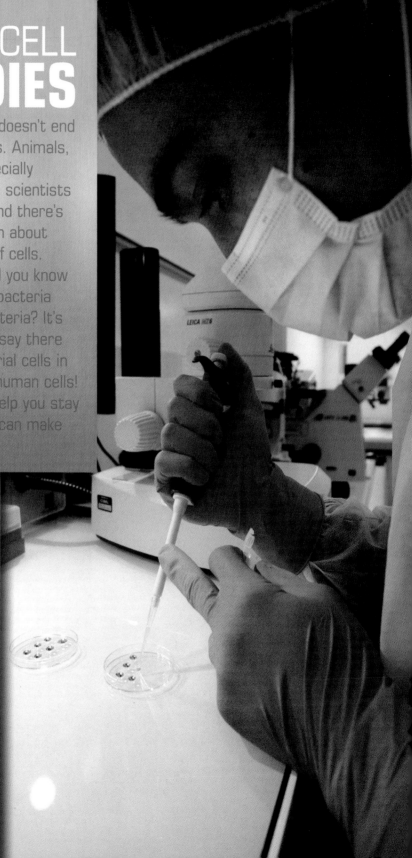

MORE CELL
STUDIES

Scientific study doesn't end with human cells. Animals, plants, and especially bacteria all have scientists hard at work. And there's a lot left to learn about different kinds of cells. For example, did you know there are good bacteria and harmful bacteria? It's true! Scientists say there are more bacterial cells in your body than human cells! Many of these help you stay healthy. Others can make you sick.

Who knows what scientists will learn about cells next?

Every time you look at a tree, your friend, or a lizard at the zoo, you're seeing countless numbers of cells at work. Scientists have studied these building blocks of organisms for hundreds of years and continue to study them today. Labs around the world look to cells for answers to questions about disease prevention and management. Many scientists wonder if stem cells could be "told" how to grow or repair a person's damaged organ. New tests can check people's DNA for illnesses they may have inherited from their parents or grandparents.

The more we learn about cells, the more we realize how amazing life is. Cells—as tiny as they are—keep our hearts beating, our brains thinking, and our lungs breathing. We'd be nothing without them!

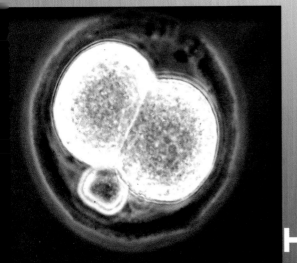

mouse cells

GLOSSARY

bacteria: tiny creatures that can only be seen with a microscope

debate: an argument or public discussion

electron: a tiny particle in atoms. An electron microscope uses a beam of electrons to create an image of a microscopic object.

genetic: relating to genes

membrane: a soft, thin layer of living matter

nutrient: something a living thing needs to grow and stay alive

pigment: a substance that gives a plant or animal color

protein: a structural material made by the body

protist: an organism belonging to the group of living things that includes bacteria and fungi

secrete: to produce and release

specimen: a sample of a group

unique: being the only one of its kind

FOR MORE INFORMATION

BOOKS

Keyser, Amber J. *The Basics of Cell Life with Max Axiom, Super Scientist*. Mankato, MN: Capstone Press, 2010.

Somervill, Barbara A. *Cells and Disease*. Chicago, IL: Heinemann Library, 2011.

Winston, Robert M. L. *Life As We Know It*. New York, NY: DK Publishing, 2012.

WEBSITES

Biology4Kids.com: Cell Structure
www.biology4kids.com/files/cell_main.html
Read more about cells and their different parts.

Cell Structures
www.neok12.com/Cell-Structures.htm
Watch videos and play games about cell structure.

INDEX